Tangled Dreams

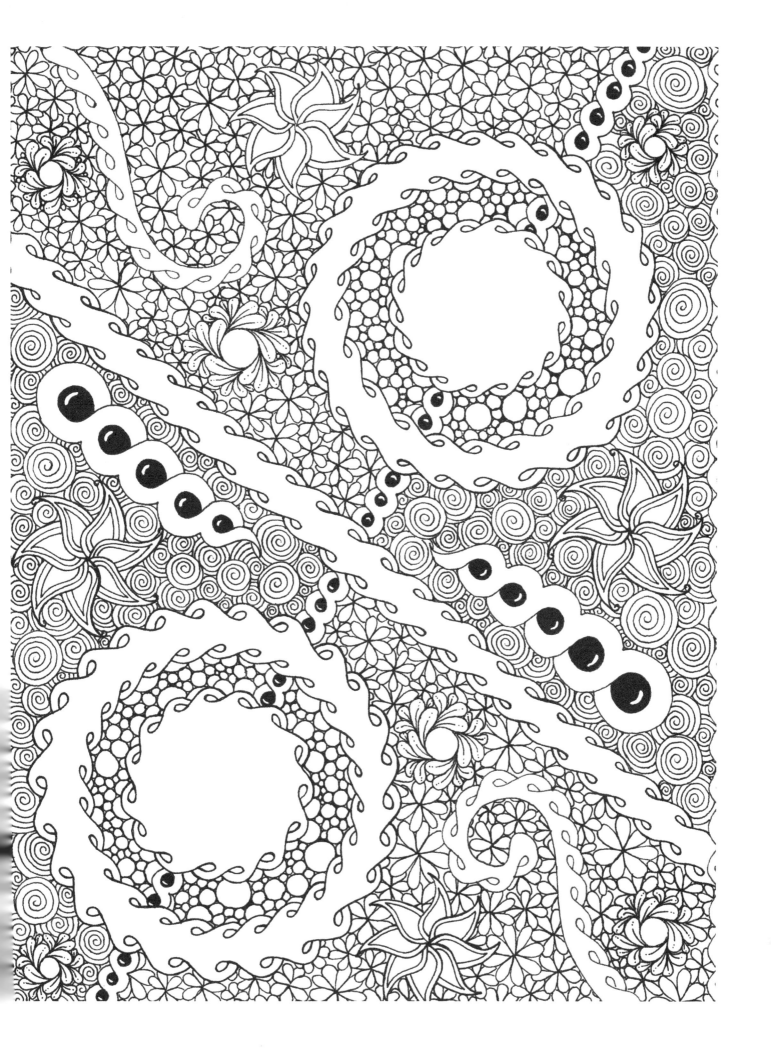

Thank you for purchasing Tangled Dreams. I hope you enjoy the designs, I certainly enjoyed drawing them. May they give you as much peace and relaxation as they have given me. I have enclosed a few blank pages for you. These can be used to test out color, practice your blending and shading before applying it to the actual piece, jot down notes, or removed and used as a protective sheet between designs. Although the quality of the paper is excellent, this may be a good idea when using "wet" mediums such as markers or gel pens. I encourage you to post your colored pages online, specifically to www.facebook.com/tabbystangledart, I love to see your coloring! Most importantly; relax, have fun, and color your heart out!

See more of Tabby's Tangled Art on the web:

Amazon : http://amzn.to/1jKtwHz

www.facebook.com/tabbystangledart

Twitter: @tabbyleann

PDF and Single Pages: https://sellfy.com/tabbyb

https://www.patreon.com/tabbyb?ty=h

Check out some awesome colorable merchandise, and well as prints from my originals and much more in my Redbubble shop!
http://www.redbubble.com/people/tabbyb

Made in the USA
Coppell, TX
15 November 2020